A YEAR OF YOU

52 NUDGES TO NAVIGATE THE NEW YEAR

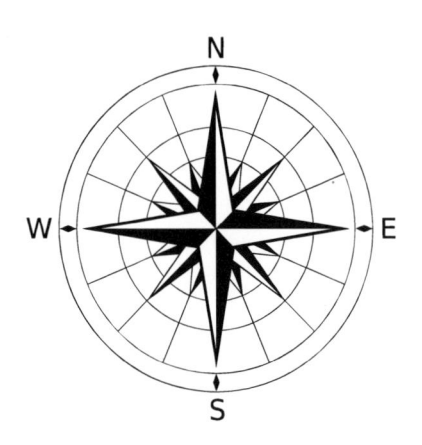

DAISY JEAN HOLLANDS

Copyright © 2023 by Daisy Jean Hollands All rights reserved. No part of this publication may be reproduced, stored or transmittedin any form or by any means, electronic, mechanical, photocopying, recording,scanning, or otherwise without written permission from the publisher. It is illegal to copy this book, post it to a website, or distribute it by any other means without permission.Daisy Jean Hollands asserts the moral right to be identified as the author of this work. First edition ISBN: 9798866434619

ACKNOWLEDGMENT

This book has been a labour of love. of hope, of frustration and tears.

There were days I thought it was going to be a walk in the park (hilarious expression to pick because if you know me, you will know how I feel about walking) and other days when I felt like it would never be finished, but here we are, it's done and I hope it helps you.

For Ben,
who showed me the rainbow.

WELCOME TO A YEAR OF YOU.

GRAB A PEN AND A NOTEBOOK, YOU ARE GOING TO WANT TO WRITE STUFF DOWN.

WE READY?

LET'S GO!

> **Aren't we lucky that every morning we are given the chance to begin again?**

New year, new start? Yes and no. It's an arbitrary date on a man-made calendar that someone in the Sixteenth Century decided would signify the beginning of the new year. As humans with freedom of thought, we get to decide when we start something new. Today might be January 1st where you are, or maybe you have picked up this book on a random Thursday in October.

The good thing is we are lucky enough to be given a new day over and over again, so when you start is entirely in your hands.

Weekly journal prompt:
It used to be thought that it takes three weeks for something to become a habit. However, more recent studies have shown that it can take up to 66 days to form a habit and up to 254 days for the habit to be cemented in our psyche. What will you start today that will be a regular part of your day by March and fully embedded by September?

> **We have to play the hand we have been given, not the cards we wish we were dealt.**

As a child from a very dysfunctional family, I spent a lot of my childhood wishing things had been different; wondering if I was adopted and my real parents would come back and rescue me. As an adult however, I became aware that you have to make the best of what you have rather than wasting time wishing for something or someone you don't.

Comparison really is the thief of joy. You won't make your own life better by wishing you were in someone else's shoes.

Weekly journal prompt:
Write down three things that bring you joy and why they make you happy. Now write down three things in your life that you wished brought you joy. Is there a way you can link the first set to the second? Can you spread the joy?

> **Show yourself the same care, kindness and consideration you would show a friend.**

You can't pour from an empty cup. I expect you have heard that saying before, but that doesn't make it any less true. There is a reason that on planes we are instructed to fit our own oxygen masks first. For most of us, the desire to help and nurture other people takes precedence over helping ourselves.

There is scope to do both, we just need to make sure we do them in the right order. Whose needs are more pressing right now?

Weekly journal prompt:
What are some of the caring things you do for other people that you never do for yourself? How can you change this so that you are practicing self-care more often?

> **Are you too close to a situation to see the bigger picture? Take a step back and adjust your focus**

When we're really close to something or when we zoom in, we can see every crack and flaw. Every speck of dust. Every fault.

We are all way too close to ourselves to get the true picture. And we hone in on the cracks and flaws instead of looking at the sum total.

If you stand a bit further back, soften your focus and widen your outlook, you get a very different view.

Weekly journal prompt:
When you zoom in on your life, which bits are magnified for you? Would your friends say the same things? Ask them what they notice most about who you are? Think about what they tell you and try to focus on those features yourself.

Call them.

Call them. Don't ask me who. You know who. As soon as you saw those two words, you knew immediately who you need to call or want to call. Instantly, their name or face flashed up in your mind.

Do it. Make that call. Life is short and we are a long time dead.

Weekly journal prompt:
Maybe you can't make the call that you would want to make. Maybe the person is no longer still with us, or maybe they are and they would refuse to take your call. Write to them instead, in your journal. It's a safe space, this is for your eyes only. Write the words you need them to hear.

> **Strive for progress, not perfection.**

When we strive for perfection, most times we are setting ourselves up for failure. And when we then fall short of our own expectations of perfection we are doing ourselves a disservice.

Instead of reaching for perfection and grasping for something we may never achieve, aim for progress. Steps towards your target. Being a better version of you today than you were yesterday

Weekly journal prompt:
Think about a time you tried and failed to be perfect. Instead of focusing on the ways you failed, list your progress. Write down all the things that went right and how those steps moved you forward.

> **Needing to be busy all the time is a trauma response.**

It really is a Twenty-First Century epidemic. Being busy all the time. It's as though people will deem us lazy or work-shy if we take our foot off the gas for a single second.

Let's examine what else is going on here. When you are filling your hours and your mind with things that you absolutely HAVE to do… what is it that you are keeping at bay?

Weekly journal prompt:
Well? What's behind that door? The one that keeping busy stops you from opening? This is a safe space. Open the door and step inside. Let's unpack.

Reach in.

Stop telling people to reach out. Sometimes, if you really want to help, you have to reach in.

Not everyone is comfortable asking for help, but at one time or another, all of us will need it.

Don't say "if there's anything I can do, just shout." They won't shout. They won't even whisper. Work out for yourself what you can do - make them a cake, collect their kids from school, go and sit in companionable silence with them.

There's always something. Reach in.

Weekly journal prompt:
Think about how you can reach in. Who do you know that is struggling, that would appreciate you reaching in?

Flip the script.

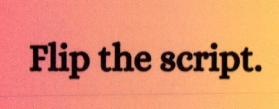

Sometimes we need to re-frame the way we look at something or change the way we verbalise it. Even the most subtle of changed can make a difference to the way we feel about something.

During the pandemic of 2020, one of the things that really helped me was, rather than thinking "we are being forced to stay indoors!" I switched to "we're lucky that we are able to stay at home"

The end result was still the same, but changing the way I spoke and thought about the situation actually made it more bearable. I wasn't feeling resentful or deprived, instead I was grateful.

Weekly journal prompt:
What is there in your life that would benefit from being looked at from a different angle? Write down your new way of looking at this.

Fact, fiction or feeling?

That thought that is nagging away in your mind, is it based in fact or fiction or feelings?

As humans we are very good at telling ourselves little stories that somehow confirm all those feelings we are having.

When you feel your thoughts running away, stop and ask yourself if the thought is based in fact or feelings. Is it something you know to be true or has your brain concocted a story to validate the feelings you are having?

Weekly journal prompt:
What's bothering you most right now? Write it down in the form of a statement and then challenge that statement - fact or feeling?

> **Your worth is not tied to your wealth, your weight, your work or your worries.**

So many of us struggle with low self-worth or self-esteem.

That's because of the way in which society generally and the patriarchy specifically have weaponized looks and bodies and even careers, setting us all up for a fall with impossible standards.

Your worth is so much more than a number on the label in the back of your jeans or the digits printed on your payslip or your bank statement and much much more than the things that keep you awake at night. You are worthy of shelter, love and respect. That is fact, it is not up for question or debate.

Weekly journal prompt:
Every day this week I want you to write
"I am worthy"
and believe it. Carry that thought with you as you go about your day.

If opportunity doesn't knock, open the door and step outside.

Sometimes we have to make our own luck, take some risks, step outside of our comfort zones, in order to make things happen.

What's worse? The pain of staying still or the pain of making a mistake? There is, of course, a third option…the one where it all works out.

Weekly journal prompt:
Think of some ways you could "step outside" and pull opportunity in. Make a list, make a plan.

Opt for reciprocity.

In friendships and in relationships, look for reciprocity.

Align yourselves to those who match your energy and give you the same things you give them.

Of course there will be times when one party is more in need than the other, but these things should level out and everyone should be getting their needs met.

There should be balance.

Weekly journal prompt:
What do you need right now? Are your needs being met in the same way you meet the needs of others?

Grab a glimmer.

Do you know what a glimmer is?
It's the opposite of a trigger. Whereas a trigger will send you spiralling, a glimmer will spark joy and comfort you.
Sometimes these are moments that will be unexpected and they will take you by surprise.
On hard days, I recommend actively seeking out your glimmers and making a point of noticing them.
The glimmers will carry you through.

Weekly journal prompt:
Think back over the past few days. What were your glimmers? Write them down and how they made you feel.

> **Once you start, you'll wish you had started sooner. Start.**

If you wait for the right time, you will never start. There will always be a reason why you can't, or you shouldn't. Let's not concern ourselves with the why nots, let's focus on the whys. Because you can. Because you want to. Because you need to.

If you want to retrain or move to a new place but your self-doubt is saying "what's the point? I'll be in my forties by the time I've finished"… well you're going to be in your forties anyway. That time is going to pass regardless, so you may as well spend it doing something you want to do.

Start.

Weekly journal prompt:
What do you want to start? What's holding you back? Write down what you want to do and the first step you are going to take towards that goal.

It is what it is.

This one had to be included after a really good friend pointed out that this is something I say a lot.

It's a very useful mantra, because acceptance is the beginning of everything. You either have to accept that something is the way it is and there's nothing you can do about it; or you have to accept that if you want things to change, you have to change things.

Acceptance leads to growth or peace and you get to decide which.

Weekly journal prompt:
What cause you most consternation in your life? Can you accept it or will you try to change it?

> **No matter how the world burns you, be sure to only radiate love.**

When we are hurting, the temptation is always to lash out, to retaliate. And sometimes that pain and anger is directed at the wrong people.

You can't fight fire with fire. When hurt comes your way, break the chain and make it stop with you. Don't become a conduit for someone else's vitriol.

It won't always be easy, but make a conscious effort to only allow love in and more importantly out of you. Deflect negativity, don't absorb it.

Weekly journal prompt:
Write down ways you can deflect pain and exude love. Maybe visualise cruel words washing over you like rainfall then the sunshine of your love dries you off. Or your love is full-body armour that keeps the arrows of pain from reaching your soft centre.

> **Measure your growth by how far you have come, not where anyone else is.**

You are not in competition with anyone else. You are just trying to be the best possible version of yourself.

So don't weigh yourself up against anyone else and decide that you aren't doing as well. Instead look at where you were then and where you are now and rejoice in the progress you have made.

Small progress is still progress. Slow progress is still progress. Celebrate your growth.

Weekly journal prompt:
My, how you've grown. Make a note of how far you have come and how good that feels.

Get comfortable with feeling uncomfortable.

Growth can be uncomfortable. Hard conversations are very uncomfortable. Telling someone "no" or "I don't want to" can feel uncomfortable to the point of impossible.

We need to push through those feelings and get used to sitting with the discomfort. Only then will things start to change and you'll start to feel the benefits of the discomfort.

After discomfort comes relief and that's when you know you are on the right track and making progress.

Weekly journal prompt:
Are there any uncomfortable conversations you need to have, or any uncomfortable feelings you need to sit with? Don't be afraid of them.

> **We all have our own way of showing love. Remember that if their way isn't your way.**

Just because someone doesn't love you the way you want to be loved doesn't mean they don't love you with everything they have.

Only you can decide if their way of loving you is enough or if you need more or different.

Some things you may be prepared to go without; the absence of some you might find unconscionable.

Weekly journal prompt:
How does being loved feel to you? Do your expectations meet your reality? If you have a partner, are they aware of your expectations? Maybe a conversation is needed.

**Tenacity
Over
Doubt
Advances
You**

If today is a bad day, t's just a day. It isn't your story. It isn't even a chapter or a page or a paragraph. It's barely a sentence and you will have the opportunity to write many more, much better sentences. There is always tomorrow. Once today is done, you never have to do today again. What can you learn from it? No day is truly wasted. Even if all you learn is that you don't want to do that again, that's progress. Find something to be grateful for. Practicing gratitude is proven to benefit mental health. There is always something. You just have to make it to bedtime. Scream, cry, shout – whatever it takes to get across the line Hold on tight You can do this. Your success rate for surviving bad days remains at 100%. Would be a terrible shame to let that record slip at this point, wouldn't it?

Weekly journal prompt:
If today is a bad day, how will you cope? What's your strategy? Write down three things that will help you get through if shit starts to go sideways.

Be present.

21st Century life can be very hectic. There is always somewhere we should be, something we are supposed to be doing and invariably there are multiple things we ought to be thinking about.

Stop.

Stop worrying about things that happened yesterday. That's gone, it's done. Stop fretting about what might happen tomorrow. That isn't here yet and tomorrow isn't promised.

All we have is the here and now, so drink it in. Don't let a second slip by unnoticed. Give the present your presence.

Weekly journal prompt:
Today just be in the moment. Sit with your journal open for ten minutes and write what is around you. Describe the room, the sounds, the way you are feeling. Notice it all and write down even the tiniest detail.

The time is now.

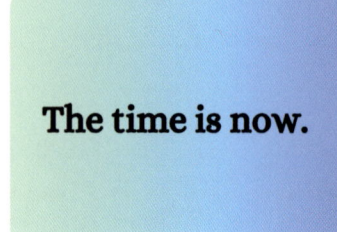

Last week we talked about being present. About being in the moment.

Yeah, about that. The time is now. What are you waiting for?

If not now, then when? If not you, then who? If not this, then what?

Don't wait for better weather, someone else's permission, or the "right" time. This is the right time and this is your sign.

Weekly journal prompt:
What are you waiting for? Write down your barriers and then cross each one of them out. We are going to find your way past them, starting today. Once you have crossed out all the reasons you can't, write down all the ways that you can and you will.

> **Embrace failure. We learn more by failing than we do when we succeed.**

It's okay to fail. It's a necessary part of the learning process. It happens to us all. You don't need to be concerned that you are failing but maybe you need to rethink how you feel about it.

Every time you get something wrong, or something doesn't work out, is an opportunity for you to do something different next time you try.

In a way, failure should be celebrated because it helps eliminate the things that don't serve you. Don't fear failure, use it as a redirect or diversion sign.

Weekly journal prompt:
Think about a time you failed. Write down the positive lessons you
learned from failing and how that helped you moving forward.

> **Sometimes we have to go backwards to go forwards.**

Not every journey will be a straight line. It's a cliche, but life really is sometimes one step forward, two steps back.
Once when I was struggling with feeling like I was going backwards, someone very wise told me to think of it as though I was an arrow being pulled back in the bow, in order to be propelled forwards at speed.
I found that super helpful and now I am passing that nugget of wisdom on to you.

Weekly journal prompt:
Are there areas of your life where you feel you are going backwards? Try to look at the bigger picture and look at ways that the backwards steps will actually help move you forwards. Write this down.

Less doing, more being.

Sometimes in life, it's okay just to be. I know there are always things that need doing and things we feel we ought to be doing. Sometimes we need to take a step back and just be.

If you can find friends with whom you can sit in comfortable silence, not doing, not saying, just being - cherish those friends. Hold onto them.

Weekly journal prompt:
Open your journal. Write "I'm going to just BE." Close your journal, close your eyes and spend ten minutes just being. Enjoy the stillness.

> **Please choose love every single day.
> Harry Styles**

To tell you the absolute truth, I could easily fill this day book with Harry Styles quotes and sayings. (And photos if I had my way!) He is very smart and eloquent and regularly imparts wisdom beyond his years. The full quote that this graphic portrays is this:

"We have a choice every single day that we wake up of what you can put into the world and I ask you to please choose love every single day."

I share the same philosophy and would always say, love more. The world needs more love, the world needs more you.

Weekly journal prompt:
How can you put a little more love into the world every day? Write "choose love" on a PostIt note and stick it somewhere you will see it every morning.

Get out of your own way.

Are you getting in your own way?Sometimes we are our own worst enemies. Fear of failure stops us from making choices and taking chances.

Asking yourself "what if it goes wrong?" and not taking action can feel like safety. You can convince yourself you are doing the right thing by not taking risks.

Asking yourself "what if it works out?" can be terrifying, because then what? You will be successful and there will be pressure from yourself and others and people will expect things of you and…and…

Stop. Get out of your own way. Trust yourself. Believe in yourself. It's going to be okay.

Weekly journal prompt:
So...are you in your own way? What are you going to do about that?

Shine bright like moonlight.

Moonlight is a special kind of magic, right? Everyone knows that. There have been poems and songs written about it, so moonlight must be something really rather wonderful, right?

Wrong.

Moonlight doesn't exist. What we perceive to be moonlight is actually a reflection of the sun.

So be like the moon, get out there and shine bright. Even on the days you don't think you can, you do - it's there in you all along.

Weekly journal prompt:
How are you going to shine today? Write it down, believe in yourself and do it.

**Choose you.
Keep choosing you.**

Choose you. It's easier said than done sometimes. When it matters, when it comes to the crunch, you really do have to choose you.

This will look different for all of us. Choose an early night. Choose to say no to toxic people. Choose boundaries and safety.

When you choose you, you are giving yourself the best chance of a more authentic existence. Choose you.

Weekly journal prompt:
How will you choose you this week? Start small, but write something down and stick to it.

Curate your space.

There are dozens of magazines about decorating your house, how to build a home you love and a garden you adore.
This isn't about feature walls or water features or how to make your kitchen cabinets pop.
This is about another space in your life. Your online space. Your feed on Instagram, on Facebook, on X (or whatever Twitter is called by the time you are reading this) on TikTok is exactly that - yours. Follow the accounts and people you want to see and read about.
The second anyone or anything makes you doubt yourself or feel bad about your own life or who you are - Unfollow. Block. Delete. You don't need to invite that into your personal space.

Weekly journal prompt:
Go do a little housekeeping on your social media feeds. Sever some ties that have been choking you and write down how good that freedom feels.

Give heartfelt compliments.

Little challenge for you. I want you to give a compliment to every person you encounter.

I don't mean you have to start stopping strangers on the street - but of course, you can if you want to!

Furthermore, I want to push you a little about the kind of compliments you give. "You look good" or "I like your shoes" aren't going to cut it.

I want you to dig a little deeper. Scratch the surface and let's find a really meaningful way to make someone's day a little brighter.

"You always know the right thing to say", "I'm proud of the way you're coping because I know things are difficult right now", "you're such a great listener" - these are all compliments that aren't based in looks.

How we look is the least interesting thing about us.

Weekly journal prompt:
You knew this was coming, didn't you? The first compliment I want you to give today is one to yourself. Write it in your journal then go look in the mirror. Look yourself right in the eye and give yourself a meaningful, heartfelt compliment.

> **Be selfish with your time. It's limited.**

I know it doesn't feel like it, but our time here is limited. The human condition is that we feel like we will live forever. It's a survival thing in a way, our brains can't or don't want to comprehend a world in which we no longer exist.

The hard truth is one day we won't and none of us knows when that day will come, so we should be very circumspect about the people we spend our precious time with while we are here.

Save your time for the people who make you feel better about yourself. The ones who make your heart happy, not your head hurt. And make sure one of those people is you. Save time for you, for yourself. It matters. You matter.

Weekly journal prompt:
If you had unlimited time, what would you be doing today? Why aren't you doing it?

> **How are you? No - how are you really?**

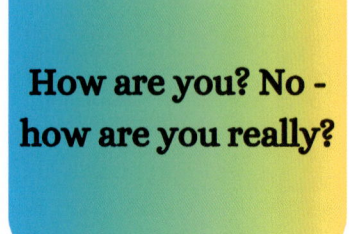

How are you? It's a simple enough question and I'm sure we all hear it often. So often that I bet you don't miss a beat or even think about how you are going to respond.
"Yeah, you know, I'm okay…"
Are you though? Just take a minute and think about how you are actually feeling.
While I'm not suggesting you take half an hour to explain how you're feeling to Janet at the watercooler in exacting detail, what I am saying is that it's a good idea to be in touch with your own feelings.
Make time and take time for you.

Weekly journal prompt:
How are you? How are you really?

Get yourself an attitude of gratitude.

Practice gratitude. Even on the bad days there is always something to be grateful for, even if that is just making it through said bad day.

Get into a grateful mindset and watch your life flourish.

Weekly journal prompt:
Write down one thing that you are grateful for. More than one thing if you can think of more, but make sure there is at least one. As you go through your week, be actively seeking things or people you are grateful for.

> **Healing isn't linear and it isn't a one way street.**

Healing is messy. It is time-consuming and sometimes all-consuming. At times you will have to go back to move forwards and there will be bumps and trip-hazards on the way.

Healing is not linear. Sometimes you will go round in circles and at times you will be so familiar with the ground that you are covering that you might be afraid you will meet yourself coming back.

All of this is normal. Healing for each of us is unique and only you will know when you are fully healed. There are no time limits or shortcuts.

Weekly journal prompt:
What are you healing from? Write down ways you can help yourself to heal and if there are things other people can help you with, write those down too.

Don't ever say "don't cry"

Crying is cathartic. It releases the stress-related hormone cortisol, as well as oxytocin and endogenous opioids, also known as endorphins. Those are feel-good chemicals which help to ease both physical and emotional pain.

Generally speaking, when someone says "don't cry", they are more concerned with their own comfort in the situation than with the feelings of the person who is crying.

Don't do that. Don't be the person who curbs or stifles someone else's emotions. Allow it. Your discomfort will pass.

If someone is prepared to let their guard down and be vulnerable in front of you, just let them cry it out.

Weekly journal prompt:
When was the last time you cried? Were you with anyone? Did they support you or did they try to shut you down? Write down how that felt.

On the days when everything seems too much., do nothing.

Sometimes life is a lot. Sometimes it can be altogether too much.

When those days come, allow them. Don't be afraid to tap out and do nothing. Give yourself a mental break.

Stay in bed. Zone out in front of re-runs of your favourite shows. And don't feel guilty about it.

Weekly journal prompt:
When was the last time you did nothing, guilt-free? Try it. Maybe just for an hour if you think a whole day is too much. Write down how it felt.

> **Don't be so focused on the destination that you overlook the journey.**

When any of us start a new venture or project, what we tend to do is envisage the end result. If you dream of winning an Oscar, for example, you think about what you might wear and the acceptance speech, the red carpet and the glittering parties afterwards. I doubt anyone is thinking about the years of drama college, the time spent in rep, the failed auditions, the part time jobs between roles to make ends meet.

We are all, at some point, guilty of focusing on the destination and overlooking the journey.

If we look more closely at the path ahead to where we want to be, we can chart our progress while we break the journey into more manageable steps.

It's good to stop occasionally, sit down and take in the scenery. If you are blinkered and honed in on the end result, you might miss something good in your peripheral. Look up once in a while.

Weekly journal prompt:
Stop and take stock for a moment. Make note of where you were and celebrate how far you have come. Write down your next steps.

> **Do you want support or do you want solutions?**

When someone comes to you with a problem or a situation in their life that is causing them consternation, the first question you should ask them is do they want support or solutions.

A lot of the time, people just need to feel seen and heard and the last thing they want to hear is " well if I were you I would…"

Maybe listen for a while. Let them unburden themselves, then wait and see if they ask for advice before you jump in.

Weekly journal prompt:
Have you ever been given unsolicited advice? How did that make you feel? Write those feelings down as a reminder to not make someone else feel that way.

> **If you have no boundaries, disrespect will walk right in.**

Boundaries are important for everyone, for you and for them.

When you set a boundary, you're sending a signal, spoken or unspoken, about how you're prepared to be treated.

Anyone who objects to you setting or having boundaries is demonstrating the exact reason you need them.

Weekly journal prompt:
What are your boundaries? Do they need redefining? Make a list, add to it often and refer back to it if you feel you are being disrespected.

> **Be real. Be vulnerable. Don't be afraid to show your flaws.**

Every single one of us is flawed. As humans, we are imperfect in myriad ways. And that's okay.

Live honestly. Don't be scared to be vulnerable and to admit your failures.

When you live authentically, and accept yourself in all your flawed glory, you enable everyone around you to do the same.

Weekly journal prompt:
Write down ways in which you are flawed. Acknowledge them. Be honest and vulnerable. What's the worst that could happen?

You have to see it before you can be it.

In order for you to make your dreams into reality. you have to first know what those dreams looks like.

Envisage yourself living your dreams. Once you can see what you want, it will be easier for you to achieve.

Weekly journal prompt:
What does your dream look like? Write it down in detail. When you imagine yourself living that dream, how do you feel? Write that down too.

> **Get out of your head, get into your life.**

What are you overthinking? We are all prone to it. Those times when we get stuck inside our heads with the what ifs and the maybes.

We talked before about fact, fiction or feeling and that is such a useful exercise, working out exactly what that thought is and what is the reality.

So which is it? Let's close the door on those thoughts for a while. Do something to distract yourself. Come back to them in a couple of hours and see how you feel.

Weekly journal prompt:
Get into the habit of journalling the things you are overthinking. And make note of whether they are fact, fiction or feeling. Once you know what the thought is, you can work out how to deal with it.

Never stop questioning.

How many times have you heard this?
"Why do we do it this way?"
"Because we've always done it this way"
Newsflash - *because we've always done it this way* - is the worst possible reason to continue doing it this way.

Follow-up questions should be: "Does this way still work?" "Is there a better way we could do this?" "Do we need to do this at all?" Maybe this way is the best way, but what if it isn't?

Weekly journal prompt:
Write down some of the key things that you do a certain way because you have always done them that way? Is that the best way, or is that habit? Is there a better way?

> **Put enough pressure into the universe and eventually it cracks open.**

There are many variations of this expression. This one was gifted to me by someone really important in my life.

There are other ways to say it. Baby steps. One day at a time. Keep on keeping on. The universe is on your side and always has your best interests at heart.

You don't have to shout about what you want, you can whisper, just keep speaking it into existence.

Weekly journal prompt:
What do you want? Ask the universe. Write it down in your journal. Write down how it will make you feel to get what you want. Come back and read what you have written on the days you feel like giving up on your dreams.

> **When we know better, we do better.**

Changing our minds on the things that matter to us is okay. In fact, I would say it's essential. As we evolve and grow as people, it's really commonplace to find that we outgrow and rethink some of our opinions and values.

And that's okay. It's way more acceptable to say "I was wrong then" than to blindly carry on living a life that isn't aligned with your current ethos.

When we know better, we do better. We are always learning and processing new information. Some outcomes will stay the same, many will change. That's how it should be.

Weekly journal prompt:
Cast your mind back five years? Ten years? How have your values and opinions changed in that time? Write that down and add that it's okay to change your mind

> **Control the things you can.
> Control how you react to the things you can't.**

Here are some of things you can control: your actions, your words, where you put your energy, how you react to other people. You can't control your emotions, but you are in control of how you deal with those emotions.

The list of things you can't control is much longer and mainly concern other people. These include such things as their opinions, their behaviours and their words.

Learn how to control how you react to the things you can't control. Be mindful of how and what you give your energy to; pause and think before you react.

Weekly journal prompt:
Go over the last few days in your mind. Make a list of the things you could control and a separate list of the things that were beyond your control. Going forward as you encounter people and situations, consider on which list they would belong.

> **Everything with intention.
> Live intentionally.**

An artist I once knew told me that when painting a picture, every single stroke of his brush was with intent. I guess I knew that this was the case with the fine detail, but I think I initially thought that some of it was just filler.

Apparently not.

It seems to me that we should live our lives in a similar manner. All things with intent.

There's a creator on TikTok, @ms_hdic that says "Go out there and have a good day in they faces on purpose!" (sic)

Salutary advice for us all. Live your best life intentionally, on purpose.

Weekly journal prompt:
What will you do on purpose and with intent today? Write it down, go do it and then come back and write how it went.

Dream big.

If you're going to have a dream, it may as well be the biggest dream possible. If you are chasing your dream, why half-ass it? Go all out. Dream as big as you can. Dream outrageous. Dream audacious. Dream without limits.

The only limits on your dreams is your imagination, so don't hold back.

Imagine winning a million pounds and your dream somehow was granted (just go along with me, it's easier to explain if you don't use words like "ridiculous" or "impossible") and the dream maker hands over your cash, saying "is that all you wanted? I have unlimited money available...if only you had dreamed of more..."

It's a dream, right? So make it as big and spectacular as you can and then if you only make a bit of it come true, it will still be incredible.

Weekly journal prompt:
You already know what this is going to be, don't you? Go on - dream big. Journal it in exacting detail.

> **Just because someone puts something down doesn't mean you have to pick it up.**

Over the course of your life, a lot of people will say a lot of things to you. Some of those things will be nice, some of them not so nice.

The good thing is you get to choose which of those you pick up and carry with you.

If someone says something particularly cruel or unkind, let it fall to the floor where it belongs and walk away. It's not yours. Don't pick it up and don't give it any of your energy or head space.

Leave it where it lands, it's not for you.

Weekly journal prompt:
Write down ten nice things people have said about you over the years. And then make a conscious effort to say something nice to someone today. Pay it forward.

The end.

Or is it?

The end.

The end of the month. The end of the year. The end of the book.

It's not really the end, you know. Every new beginning stems from something that has ended.

Aren't we lucky that every morning we wake up with the knowledge that we get to start over?

Weekly journal prompt:
What were your highlights? Of the week, the month, the year, the book?
Look back over your journal and see which days resonated most with you. I'd love to know!

IF YOU HAVE MADE IT TO THE END, THANK YOU.

THANK YOU FOR SHOWING UP AND COMMITTING SOME TIME TO BEING THE BEST VERSION OF YOU POSSIBLE THIS YEAR.

SHALL WE DO IT ALL AGAIN NEXT YEAR?

YOU CAN FIND ME ON INSTAGRAM
@THEDAILYDAISY_MOTIVATION

Printed in Great Britain
by Amazon